La Grande

Oregon Trail

Wallowa

Mountains

Hells Canyon

Powder River

Halfway

Snake River

...NTAINS

...MPTER

Baker City

BUCKY'S GOLD

DEDICATION

To all the dedicated and generous people who made
Salem's Riverfront Carousel come to life;

To Elaine for sharing her creative ideas and skills;

And to Bill for teaching me so much about horses.

Special thanks to Don Wegner and Bill & Gail Bonniksen,
whose generous donations financed the publication of this book.

Published by
Little America Publishing Company®
(an imprint of Beautiful America Publishing Company®)
P.O. Box 244, 2600 Progress Way
Woodburn, OR 97071

Library of Congress Catalog Number 2002074685
ISBN 0-89802-698-9

BUCKY'S GOLD

WRITTEN AND ILLUSTRATED
BY JANEE HUGHES

It started out just an ordinary spring day, his third in a corral behind the Baker City Livery Stable. Bucky couldn't have known that what was about to happen would change his life forever. He was getting bored so he was examining the gate latch and trying to figure out how to open it with his teeth when two men approached.

He recognized the big one with the bushy beard, Jeb. But the smaller, skinnier one was new to him. His face was covered with sweat and dust, and he walked with a slight limp. "I've got to have a good, strong horse. I need to get to the Blue Mountains so I can start prospecting for gold," the stranger said to Jeb.

"You and everybody else, Tom," replied Jeb. "This here pinto is all I've got. The best horses went fast when the news of a gold discovery got around."

Knowing that he was not included among the "best horses" did nothing to improve Bucky's attitude. He didn't like people much, anyway, so when the new man, Tom, opened the gate and walked up to him, he laid back his ears and gave him a sour look.

"You mean this is the best you can do? This is about the ugliest horse I've ever seen! He's rough and shaggy, he's got mean little eyes, and what's the matter with his teeth? They stick out and one of them's broken off. Looks like it's rubbing his lip sore, too."

Bucky switched his tail at the insult. It reminded him of the time that crazy cowboy got so mad he came after him with a club! Some people have no sense of humor. Bucky slyly stepped sideways, aiming to land on Tom's foot, but the scrawny cowboy moved just in time.

Jeb shrugged his shoulders. "His name's Bucky. He's sound and fit, and his bad teeth won't affect his legs. The way I see it, you don't have much choice. You can wait for your lame horse to get better, or you can trade straight across for this one."

"You don't have *anything* else?"

"Nope."

"I'll take him," Tom sighed. "I don't want to walk any farther. Maybe you'll have something better I can trade him for next time I'm in town."

Bucky watched Tom limp away and then return with a saddle and bridle. Good! He was going to have a little fun today, after all. He'd show this hot-shot cowboy a thing or two!

Then Jeb spoke up. "By the way, I'm not sure he was called Bucky because of his teeth."

"What did you say?"

Jeb grinned. "Oh, never mind. You'll figure it out soon enough."

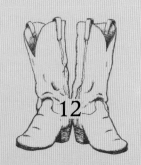

Tom caught Bucky, tied him to a post, and threw on the saddle. As Bucky felt the cinch tighten up, he rolled his eyes and humped his back. Then Tom untied him. With a grunt, Bucky wheeled around and sprang into the air. He twisted his body and snapped his hind legs up high as he came down on stiff front legs. Bellowing, he bucked around and around the corral, stirring up a cloud of dust. Finally, pleased with his performance, he stopped to catch his breath.

"Oh, great!" Tom said. "You could have mentioned this little defect. But I won't back out of the deal. He isn't the first bronc I've ridden."

Bucky saved his energy as Tom tied him to the post, traded a bridle for the halter and tied saddle bags and a bedroll behind the saddle. He pulled down his hat and jumped on.

Bucky didn't get his reputation for nothing, and he did his best to prove it. He jumped high in the air, threw his head down, and let out a bellow. Then he hit the ground hard and leaped up again, this time twisting around in mid-air. When he hit the ground the second time, he was surprised that Tom was still in the saddle, but he figured the man wouldn't last more than another jump or two. He bucked around and around the corral, but the new cowboy stuck to the saddle like a burr. This guy was *good*!

"Open the gate!" Tom yelled to Jeb. Bucky spotted the opening and went tearing through it and out onto Main Street. Men yelled, dogs barked, and women gathered up their children as Tom and Bucky bucked their way down the street. They passed the last plank building and Bucky was getting very tired. That darn cowboy was *still there*! Reluctantly, he decided to let the cowboy think he had the upper hand. He gave one final hop and broke into a trot.

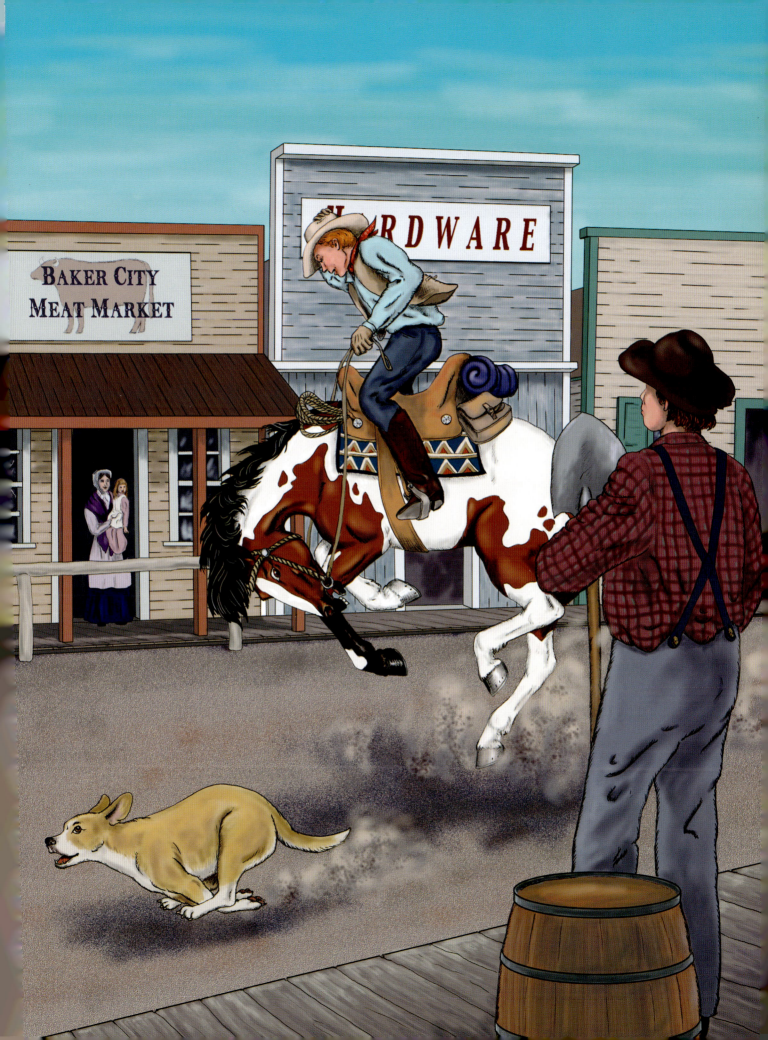

They kept right on going, heading up into the mountains. Bucky still wasn't happy about carrying a rider, but it was hard to buck while moving at a fast pace over a rough trail. Finally, they stopped beside a clear, cold stream and spent the night. There was plenty of good, sweet grass, a big improvement over the moldy hay provided by the livery stable.

For the next two weeks, Bucky carried Tom higher and higher into the mountains. Each morning when Tom first mounted, Bucky did his best to unseat him with a few good bucks. He knew there had to be a way to get the best of this guy. He was surprised, though, that Tom never got mad at him. It was almost as if he enjoyed it. They stopped often and Tom panned for gold in the little creeks. Bucky ate sweet meadow grass and enjoyed the sunny days and clear mountain air.

Then one afternoon, Tom sounded very discouraged as they rode along. "I've got to find something pretty soon, Bucky," he said, "or go back empty handed. I'm out of food, and I don't have enough money to buy much if we do go back to town." He seemed distracted in his misery. Being just naturally ornery, Bucky couldn't resist. As they started across a small stream, he let loose with one of his best bucks. It took Tom by surprise and he went flying over Bucky's head and hit the water with a splash.

He had finally done it! Bucky savored the moment as he watched Tom sit up and grab for his hat.

"Doggone it, Bucky, that was uncalled for!" he sputtered, dumping water out of his hat. "I thought we had an understanding!"

Bucky put on his most innocent, surprised look as Tom walked over and bent down to pick up the reins. Then he paused and reached into the gravel to pick up a shiny rock. He turned it over in his hands. It had a soft, warm glow, different than any other rocks Bucky had seen. Tom suddenly threw his wet hat in the air and yelled, "Gold! Whoopee! We're rich, Bucky! Looks like you did me a favor dumping me right here on top of it!"

Tom quickly tied Bucky to a tree and ran back to the stream with his gold pan. He spent the whole afternoon filling a leather pouch with more of the gold. He didn't seem to notice that it was getting cloudy and a lot colder. Finally, as it was starting to get dark, he came back and put the heavy pouch in the saddle bag.

Just then Bucky felt the first cold, wet flakes of snow. Tom pulled his collar up around his ears and led the pinto to a sheltered spot under some trees. As the snow continued to fall, Bucky watched Tom whooping and hopping around the fire, stopping frequently to gaze at the nuggets he held in his fists.

Bucky didn't sleep much that night. The wind grew colder and the snow fell harder. Tom kept getting up to add fuel to the fire. By morning, Bucky was shivering and he knew they were in real danger. Tom must have felt the same. Smoothing out the saddle blanket, he said, "Bucky, we have to get out of here! All this gold isn't going to do us any good if we freeze to death."

Tom threw on the saddle and mounted, and Bucky only bucked two feeble jumps to get his muscles limbered up. Then he headed down the canyon. He was as eager to get out of those mountains as Tom, but by now the snow was deep and it was rough going. It was hard work plowing through the deep drifts, and once, the trail was blocked by trees that had blown down in the storm. Bucky had to climb up the side of a canyon to find a way past the windfall. Tom wisely let him find his own way up the steep incline and over the icy rocks. At last, as the light began to fade, the canyon widened and the ground flattened out.

26

Bucky couldn't remember ever being so tired. He felt stabs of pain in his empty stomach. As Tom unsaddled him and tied him under some trees, he left the saddle blanket in place, and Bucky was glad of its scant protection. Tom must have been very cold, too, because he stood for a long time warming his hands under Bucky's mane. "Bucky," he said, "I'm sorry there's nothing for you to eat. And I'm sorry I wanted to get rid of you because of your teeth. I was wrong about you. You're the best horse I've ever owned."

No one had ever said anything like *that* to Bucky before! Suddenly the cold, fatigue, and hunger didn't seem so bad.

Tom and Bucky spent another night fighting to stay warm. By morning, the snow had stopped and the sky was clear, but it was very cold. Bucky was shivering as Tom saddled him. Tom led him down the canyon, and when they reached a patch of wind-swept grass, Bucky ate eagerly while Tom fished in the stream. The sun grew warmer and the snow began to melt while Tom cooked and ate his catch.

When Bucky had eaten his fill, Tom climbed in the saddle. Bucky looked back at him, but he was just too tired to buck. "Poor guy," Tom said softly, "I know this has been really hard on you, but I think we're through the worst of it now. You saved my life, Bucky, and I thank you. Wish I could find a way to make it up to you."

Two days later they made it to Baker City. Their first stop was a feed store, where Tom made sure Bucky had a good meal of oats. Then they went to the other end of town where Tom tied Bucky in front of a plank building. He went inside and returned with a heavy-set man dressed in a thin white jacket.

"You're a dentist, Dr. Bonny, and it shouldn't be much different for horses," Tom said, "I've got plenty of gold."

Dr. Bonny looked in Bucky's mouth and nodded, "Bring him around back."

"Now, behave yourself, Bucky," Tom said when they were behind the building, "Dr. Bonny is going to help you."

Bucky didn't like that strange man working in his mouth *at all*! But it didn't hurt, so he just warned the doctor to be careful by switching his tail and stomping his foot now and then. Finally, Dr. Bonny and Tom stepped back and smiled. Then Bucky caught a glimpse of his reflection in a window. Amazing! He had a new tooth where the old broken one had been, and it was shiny gold! He looked handsome, and rich!

He arched his neck and pranced proudly as Tom rode him over to the General Store. He could see the gleam of his new tooth reflecting in the windows. As Tom tied him up he grinned and said, "Bucky, I bet you're the only horse in the world with a gold tooth! But you earned it."

Several people coming out of the store gathered around, admiring Bucky's beautiful new smile. Most of them, that is. One man asked, "Why would anyone in his right mind put all that gold into a horse's mouth?" Bucky gave him a sour look.

"This is no ordinary horse," Tom answered. "He's the one that found the gold in that tooth, and he saved my life, too!"

Soon the crowd broke up and Tom walked into the store. But Bucky noticed a shifty-eyed man lingering around the corner of the building. Once Tom was out of sight, the man dashed over and untied the reins. Bucky rolled his eyes and flattened his ears at him, but the stranger didn't seem to notice. Bucky felt the man's weight as he swung into the saddle and then the sting of his spurs.

Bucky wasn't about to take that! Nobody was going to take him away from Tom! He let out a bellow and gave that stranger a fine demonstration of his famous, spine-twisting bucks.

Bucky proudly trotted back to the hitching rail, shaking his head so that the gold tooth sparkled.

Tom stepped out of the store, laughing hard. "Mister, you sure picked the wrong horse!" he said, "Did I mention his name is *Bucky*?"

ABOUT SALEM'S RIVERFRONT CAROUSEL

In 1996, Hazel Patton visited Missoula, Montana, where she saw the first old-world style carousel built in the U.S. since the Great Depression. She also saw how this volunteer project had united and inspired the community. Her vision was to bring a similar project to Salem.

Hazel's inspiration and enthusiasm spread. Donations of time, expertise, and money began to pour in. Under the capable direction of Dave and Sandy Walker, hundreds of volunteers carved and painted a total of 43 beautiful horses, as well as the many other components of the carousel. Finally, the finished carousel was housed in a beautiful new building designed especially for the carousel and placed in Riverfront Park.

Each of the carousel horses is unique, designed according to the wishes of families and businesses who "adopted" it. Many are an inspiration to artists, writers and musicians.

All of the volunteers invite you to visit Salem's Riverfront Carousel. Climb up on Bucky or one of the other hand-carved steeds, and when the organ music begins, hang on and enjoy a magical ride!

ABOUT THE AUTHOR AND ILLUSTRATOR

Janee Hughes spent 31 years teaching art in middle school. Since retiring she has pursued a free lance art career. She has illustrated magazines, newspapers, and catalogs, and has won awards for her equine paintings. She also enjoys writing, and has had articles published in equine magazines.

Janee was a dedicated volunteer on the Carousel project. She was a member of the team that painted the horses, and she also painted many of the shields. Then she joined the writer's committee and began working on books.

Although she usually works in watercolors and acrylics, Janee enjoys the flexibility of the computer for illustrating books. She scans her original drawings, then uses a painting program to complete them. This is the third book she has illustrated this way.

Janee and her husband Bill have always enjoyed horses. They have ridden many miles of trails in Oregon's wilderness areas. They live east of Salem where they can enjoy their horses and dogs.

PENDLETON

BLUE MO

UKIAH

NORTHEASTERN OREGON 1870

PRAIRIE CITY

JOHN DAY